WRITING THAT CHANGED U.S. HISTORY

EMANCIPATION PROCLAMATION

by Josephine Larsen

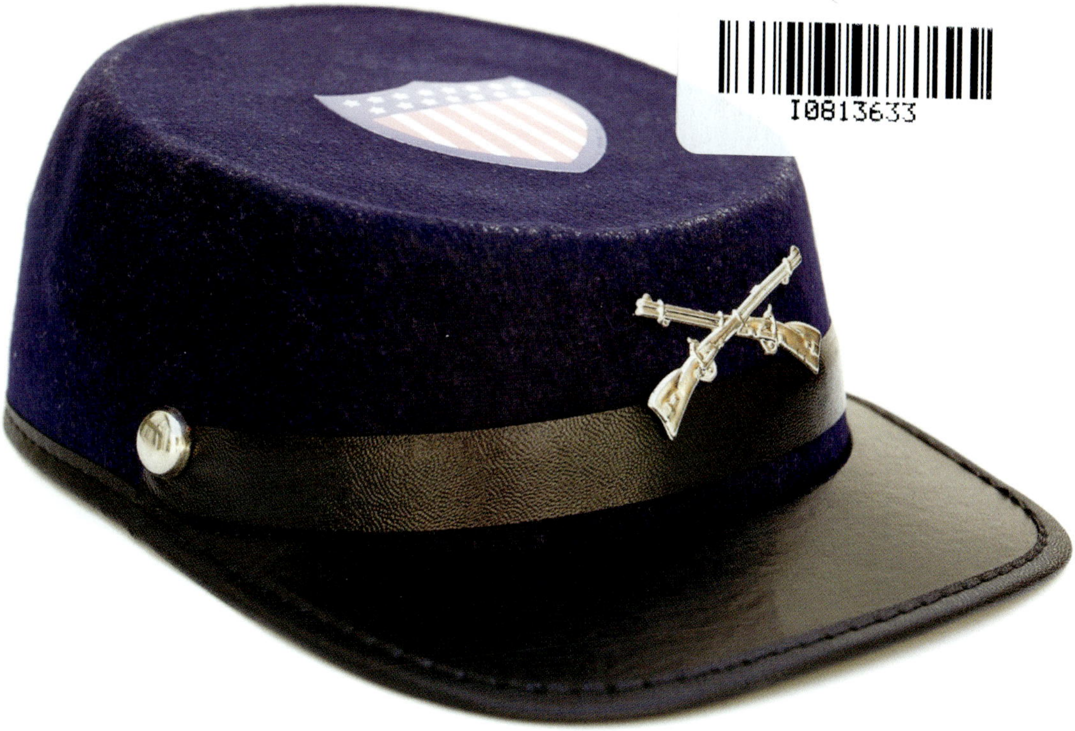

Pogo Books, an imprint of Jump! Library by FlutterBee

Ideas for Parents and Teachers

Pogo Books let children practice reading informational text while introducing them to nonfiction features such as headings, labels, sidebars, maps, and diagrams, as well as a table of contents, glossary, and index.

Carefully leveled text with a strong photo match offers early fluent readers the support they need to succeed.

Before Reading

- "Walk" through the book and point out the various nonfiction features. Ask the student what purpose each feature serves.
- Look at the glossary together. Read and discuss the words.

During Reading

- Have the child read the book independently.
- Invite them to list questions that arise from reading.

After Reading

- Discuss the child's questions. Talk about how they might find answers to those questions.
- Prompt the child to think more. Ask: What did the Emancipation Proclamation accomplish? Do you think it could have done more? Why?

Pogo Books are published by Jump!
3500 American Blvd W, Suite 150
Bloomington, MN 55431
www.jumplibrary.com

Jump! is a division of FlutterBee Education Group.

Library of Congress Cataloging-in-Publication Data

Names: Larsen, Josephine author
Title: Emancipation proclamation / by Josephine Larsen.
Description: Bloomington, MN: Jump!, Inc., [2026]
Series: Writing that changed U.S. history | Includes index
Audience: Ages 7-10
Identifiers: LCCN 2025029914 (print)
LCCN 2025029915 (ebook)
ISBN 9798896623496 hardcover
ISBN 9798896623502 paperback
ISBN 9798896623519 ebook
Subjects: LCSH: United States. President (1861-1865: Lincoln).
Emancipation Proclamation–Juvenile literature
Enslaved persons–Emancipation–United States–Juvenile literature | United States–History–Civil War, 1861-1865–Participation, African American–Juvenile literature
Classification: LCC E453 .L28 2026 (print)
LCC E453 (ebook)
LC record available at https://lccn.loc.gov/2025029914
LC ebook record available at https://lccn.loc.gov/2025029915

Editor: Alyssa Sorenson
Designer: Emma Almgren-Bersie

Photo Credits: Library of Congress, cover (document), 4, 5, 10, 18, 19; mato181/Shutterstock, cover (flag); Noel V. Baebler/Shutterstock, 1; Bjoern Wylezich/iStock, 3; Kurz & Allison-Art Studio/American History Museum/Smithsonian, 6-7; Ed Vebell/Getty, 8-9; North Wind Picture Archives/Alamy, 12-13; Wikimedia, 14-15; Everett Collection/Shutterstock, 16-17; Richard Levine/Alamy, 20-21; Onur ERSIN/Shutterstock, 23.

Printed in the United States of America at
Corporate Graphics in North Mankato, Minnesota.

TABLE OF CONTENTS

CHAPTER 1

A DIVIDED COUNTRY

By the 1800s, Black people had been **enslaved** in North America for more than 200 years. White slaveholders forced them to work on **plantations**. It was hard work. They were not paid. Slaveholders hurt them.

Northern U.S. states made slavery **illegal** in the early 1800s. In 1861, Abraham Lincoln became president. He was from the North. People in the South were worried. Why? They thought he would make slavery illegal in the South.

Southern states formed their own country. They called it the Confederacy. States in the North were called the Union. The Union wanted the country to stay together. The two sides fought. This was the American Civil War (1861–1865).

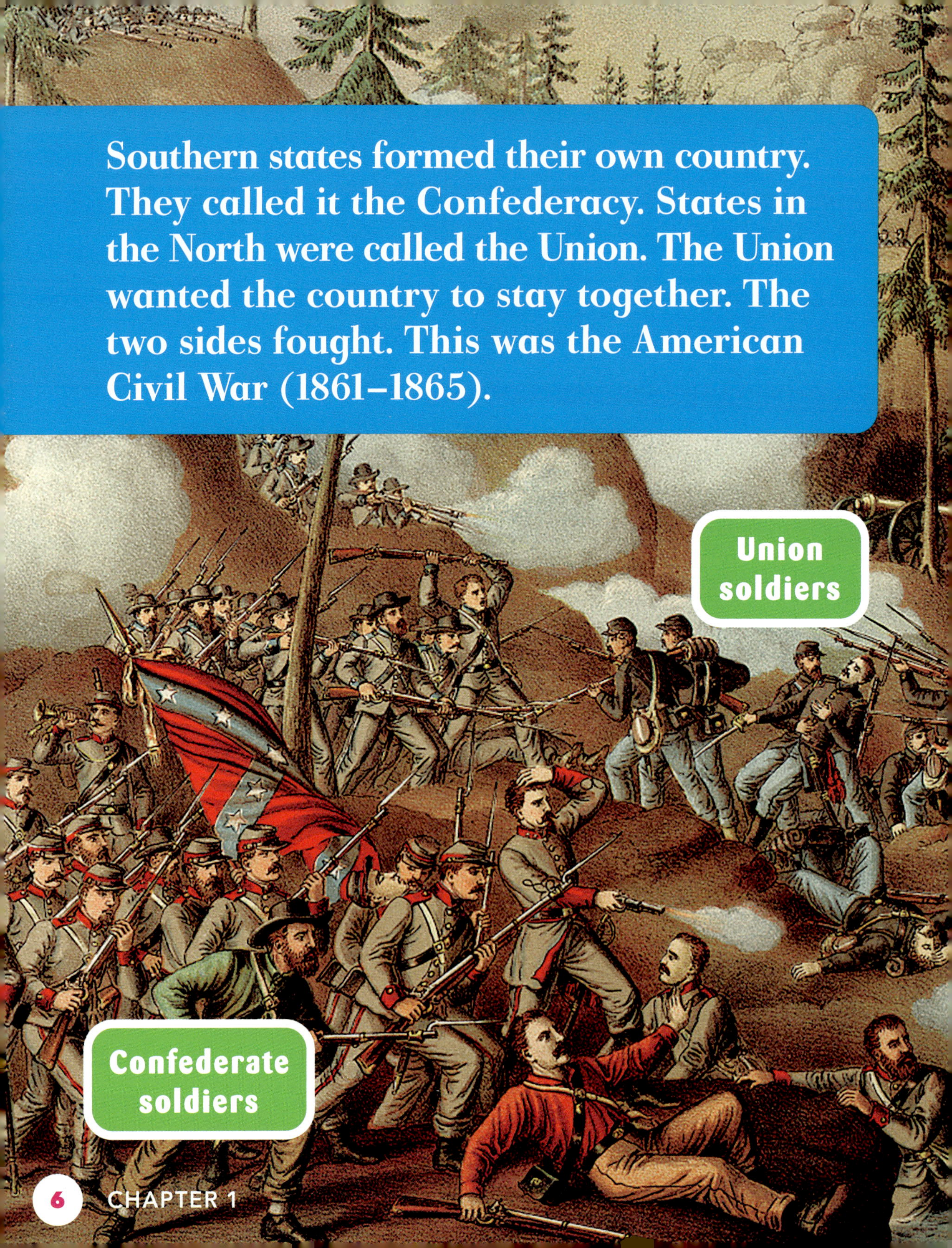

TAKE A LOOK!

Which states were part of the Confederacy? Which were part of the Union? Take a look.

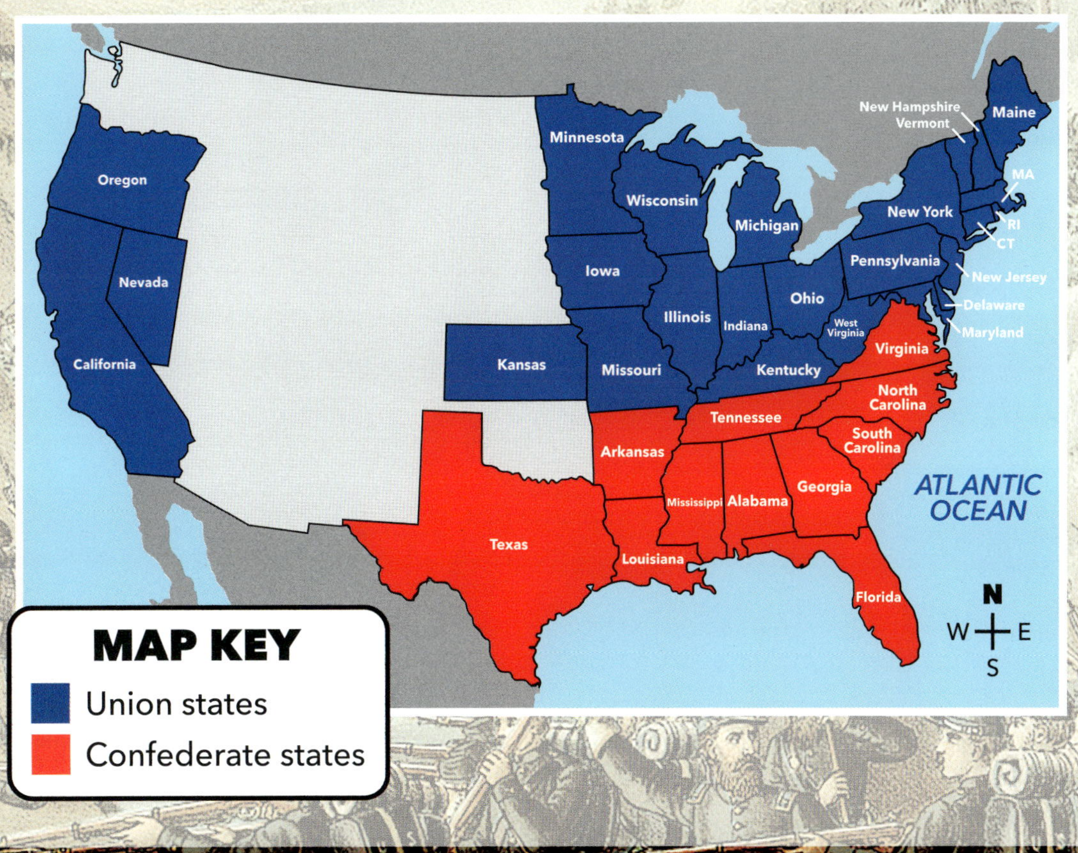

Lincoln wanted to keep the United States together. But the war dragged on. He needed to **inspire** people in the Union to keep fighting. He wanted to give enslaved people hope for freedom. He started writing a **proclamation**.

CHAPTER 2

THE PROCLAMATION

On January 1, 1863, Lincoln shared his new document with the public. It was called the **Emancipation** Proclamation. It said enslaved people in the Confederate states were free. They had to be paid for their work.

Slavery still took place in some Union states. These were called border states. They could keep people enslaved. Why? Lincoln did not want to make them mad. He worried they would join the Confederacy.

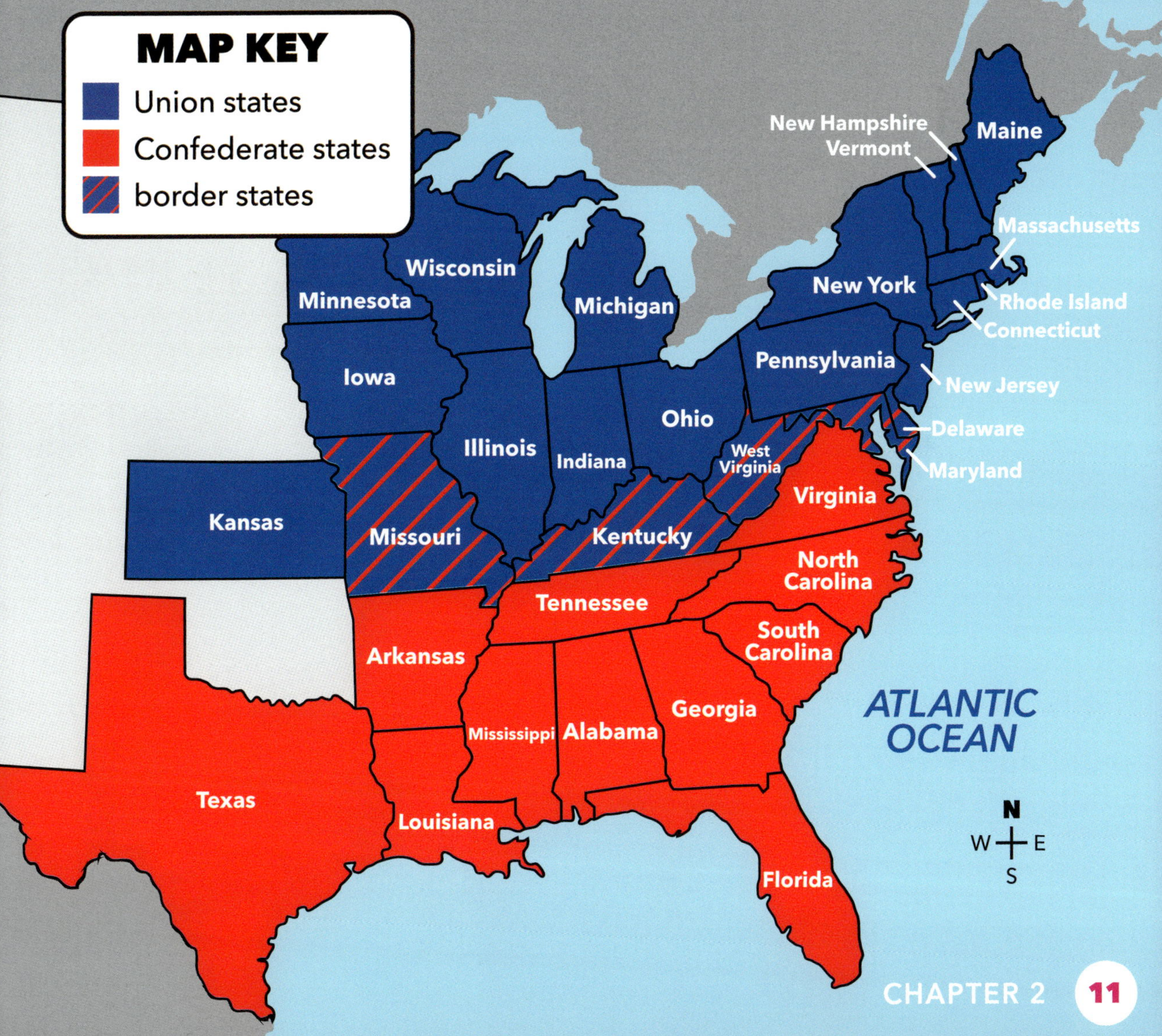

Confederate leaders did not see Lincoln as their president. They did not follow the Proclamation. They did not tell enslaved people they were free.

The war continued. Union soldiers won battles. They took land in the South. Soldiers saw enslaved people. They told them they were free.

freed people

The Proclamation said Black men could be soldiers for the Union. Black men from the North and freed men from the South joined. They wanted to fight for freedom. They helped the North win more battles.

DID YOU KNOW?

Almost 200,000 Black soldiers joined the Union. Many fought. They also worked as nurses, doctors, and spies.

The Proclamation made freedom the most important issue in the Civil War. Other countries would not help the South because of it. Why? They did not want to work with people who had slaves. Without help, the South became weaker.

WHAT DO YOU THINK?

People still talk about the Emancipation Proclamation. Do you think it is important to learn about this document? Why or why not?

54TH MASS

CHAPTER 3

FREEDOM FOR ALL

The North won the war in April 1865. The South became part of the United States again. Many people celebrated. How? Some cities had parades.

Thirteenth Amendment

Thirty-Eighth Congress of the United States.

A Resolution: Submitting to the Legislatures of the several States a proposition to amend the Constitution of the United States.

Resolved by the Senate and House of Representatives of the United States of America in Congress assembled, (two-thirds of both Houses concurring) That the following article be proposed to the Legislatures of the several States as an amendment to the Constitution of the United States, which, when ratified by three-fourths of said Legislatures, shall be valid, to all intents and purposes, as a part of the said Constitution, namely:

ARTICLE XIII.

Section 1. Neither slavery nor involuntary servitude, except as a punishment for crime, whereof the party shall have been duly convicted, shall exist within the United States, or any place subject to their jurisdiction.

Section 2. Congress shall have power to enforce this article by appropriate legislation.

Attest:

Secretary of the Senate

Clerk of the House of Representatives

Speaker of the House of Representatives

H. Hamlin Vice President of the United States and President of the Senate

Approved, February 1. 1865. Abraham Lincoln

In the Senate April 8. 1864.

In the House of Representatives January 31. 1865.

At the end of the war, the Thirteenth **Amendment** was added to the U.S. **Constitution**. It made slavery illegal everywhere in the United States.

JUNETEENT
CELEBRATIC

It took more than two years for all enslaved people in the South to know they were free thanks to the Proclamation. The news did not reach parts of Texas until June 19, 1865. The United States celebrates this **anniversary** with a holiday. It is called Juneteenth. The Proclamation made freedom for all possible.

WHAT DO YOU THINK?

Juneteenth has been celebrated since 1866. It became an official holiday in 2021. It took more than 150 years for the government to recognize it. Should it have been sooner? What do you think?

QUICK FACTS & TOOLS

TIMELINE

What are important dates in the history of the Emancipation Proclamation? Take a look!

MARCH 4, 1861
Abraham Lincoln becomes president.

APRIL 12, 1861
The Battle of Fort Sumter in South Carolina starts the Civil War.

JANUARY 1, 1863
Lincoln shares the Emancipation Proclamation.

APRIL 9, 1865
The Union wins the Civil War.

DECEMBER 6, 1865
The Thirteenth Amendment says slavery is illegal in the United States.

GLOSSARY

amendment: A change made to a law or legal document.

anniversary: A date that people remember each year because of an important event that happened on that date in an earlier year.

Constitution: A written document that says how the United States should be run.

emancipation: The act of freeing people from slavery.

enslaved: Forced to work in harsh conditions with no pay.

illegal: Against the law.

inspire: To influence or encourage someone to do something.

plantations: Large farms in warm climates on which crops, such as coffee beans and cotton, are grown.

proclamation: An announcement.

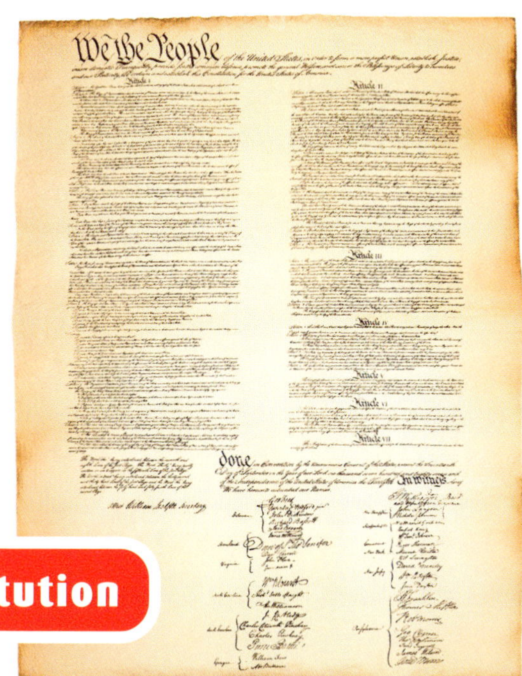

U.S. Constitution

INDEX

TO LEARN MORE

Finding more information is as easy as 1, 2, 3.

1. Go to www.factsurfer.com
2. Enter "Emancipation Proclamation" into the search box.
3. Choose your book to see a list of websites.